# Volcano!

by Gillian Clements

## Contents

| | |
|---|---|
| The "Emerald Isle" | 2 |
| The volcano wakes up | 4 |
| The "Day of Death" | 6 |
| After the eruption | 8 |
| Anger | 10 |
| Could the government have done more? | 12 |
| Could scientists have done more? | 14 |
| Loss and grief | 16 |
| Shelters | 18 |
| The old and the ill | 20 |
| New homes | 22 |
| The plight of the farmers | 24 |
| Exile | 26 |
| Life in Britain | 28 |
| The future for the "Emerald Isle"? | 30 |
| Index | 32 |

# The "Emerald Isle"

Montserrat is a tiny island in the Caribbean. The island was formed hundreds of years ago, when a volcano rose up from the seabed. Montserrat was so green that the island people called it the "emerald isle".

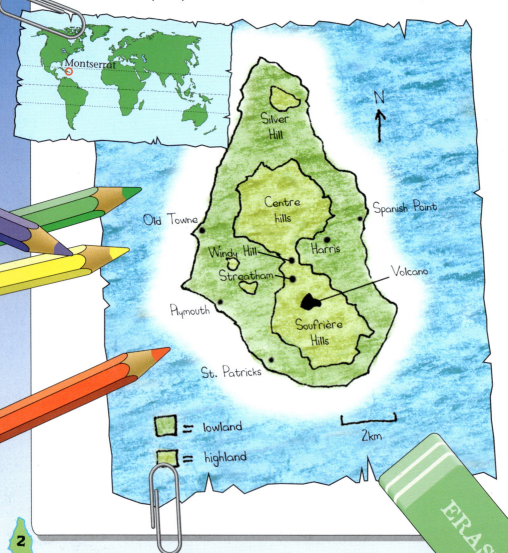

Eleven thousand people lived safely and peacefully, mostly in the south of the island. Some were farmers. They grew mangoes, guavas and vegetables, and kept their animals on the hills. Some worked for the government in Plymouth, the capital of the island. Others lived and worked in small villages. Most people had nice houses, and a good life.

A farmer at work.

Montserrat was a very green island.

The town of Plymouth.

The volcano was not extinct but it had been peaceful for over three hundred years. Then, in 1995, it began to wake up.

# The volcano wakes up

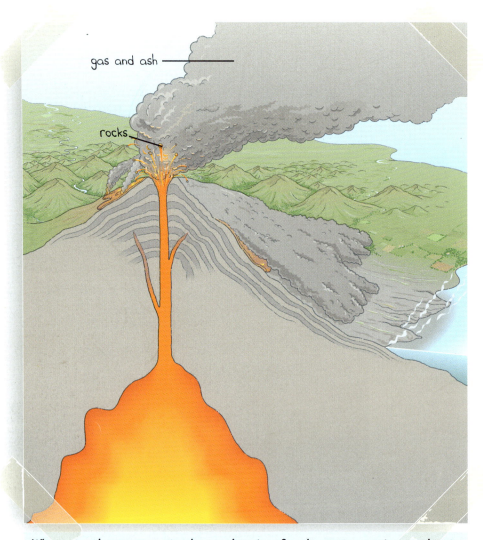

When a volcano erupts, huge clouds of ash, rocks and gas shoot out of the crater at the top. Then the clouds rush down the hill slopes on to people and land below.

In 1995 the volcano woke up. First it sent steam and ash high up above the green Soufrière Hills. Scientists from islands close by and from America came to the island to see what was happening. They measured the ground. Liquid rock (called lava) underground was making it rise up like a dome.

The scientists couldn't tell whether the volcano was really going to explode, or if it would simply spit out ash for a while. Volcanoes often rumble for years without erupting.

But this volcano did erupt. On Monday, 23 June 1997 a huge cloud filled the sky and dropped ash like rain on Plymouth. Then the volcano showered red-hot rocks over the island. The people said the rocks were big enough to crush a roof. Some rocks set buildings on fire.

That day became known as "Ash Monday".

The island people were frightened. Six thousand of them were told to move north to escape the volcano. Some moved. Others left the island for a safer place.

The volcano errupting.

# The "Day of Death"

The islanders call Tuesday, 24 June 1997 the "Day of Death". There was a sound like jet engines. There was thunder and lightning. Then boiling clouds of ash and rocks rushed down the steep sides of the volcano.

The ash clouds were deadly.

People had been told to leave their homes after the volcano's first rumblings. But some came back for a few hours now and then to feed their animals and look after their crops. Now the ash clouds rolled down towards them. Inside each cloud, it was hotter than an oven. Anything caught by the clouds was burnt to cinders. A baby, her mother, old men, farmers … people in their cars and homes. No one in the cloud's path could escape.

Nineteen people died in just a few minutes.

# After the eruption

People told their escape stories.
One of the islanders said,
"It was like a burning hurricane!
There was no warning!"

It moved very fast, very, very fast. The boiling ash was in big clumps.

Another islander, Delia Ponde, told how an ash cloud followed her, her husband and child as they drove at top speed down the hillside.

Then the islanders looked to see what was left. Grey ash covered Plymouth and all of western Montserrat. The wind had carried it there. Around them, the people could see terrible destruction. The south and east of their green island had been buried under metres of molten rock. Villages like Harris and Windy Hill had gone.

Plymouth was covered in ash.

Molten rock and volcanic ash buried villages.

The people of Montserrat were shocked. What could be done with their ruined island?

# Anger

For some islanders, shock turned to anger. They thought that the scientists and politicians should have told them more about the danger they were in. They hadn't understood that the volcano could be so dangerous – they had never seen it erupt before.

Angry islanders on the street in Montserrat.

But the scientists and politicians were not totally to blame. Many islanders had not wanted to hear bad news. They had been warned to move away. They had seen their green fields turn grey with ash, and some cattle had died even before the "Day of Death". They did not really understand how much danger they were in, or that the danger would last a long time. Some old people had not wanted to leave their village homes, and some of them went back to their homes before it was safe for them to do so. One old farmer, Joseph Browne, who lived in Streatham, stayed one night in a shelter, but then went back to his home. Sadly, he was killed when burning ash fell on him.

Instruments are used to record the amount of activity detected by sensors around the volcano.

Burning ash continued to fall on the island.

# Could the government have done more?

Montserrat is ruled by the British government, thousands of miles away. When the volcano began to rumble, some islanders thought that the British rulers were too far away and didn't care enough about what happened on the island. Some thought that the government did not do enough to prepare the island for the disaster. Were people warned about the possible eruption early enough?

## THEY DON'T CARE!

Could shelters have been ready for the people any sooner?

After the disaster, there were arguments over the money that was needed to build new schools, hospitals and houses.

But in 1998, the British government gave Montserrat money to start rebuilding. There was lots to do, and progress was slow, but at least it was a start.

# Could scientists have done more?

Some people thought scientists did not speak to the islanders enough to warn them about the danger. But the scientists did not know whether the volcano would erupt. If they had given the islanders information that turned out to be wrong, they would have made the people panic for no reason.

The scientists did what they thought was best.

"We watched Montserrat's volcano. The ground was lifting, and we knew it was dangerous. The **Montserrat Volcano Observatory** told the government where it was risky for the people to stay." The island's governor, Frank Savage, used this information to make new plans to be ready for any disaster.

The Montserrat Volcano Observatory advises the government on volcanic activity in Montserrat.

The Montserrat British Governor, Frank Savage, spoke to reporters about making new plans.

# Loss and grief

When their anger left them, the islanders became very sad. Many families were split up by what had happened. Older islanders went to live in tents or shelters in the north of the island. Younger ones left the island to make a new life for themselves somewhere else.

Many people simply left the island.

Many people lost their homes, their work and their money. People lost their friends. Some people became ill from breathing in the ash, but they could not be looked after at the hospital in Plymouth because it had been buried by the volcano.

Schools were used as hospitals.

The islanders who stayed on Montserrat had to take money and food from the government. They were very unhappy doing this because they were used to growing their own food and paying for what they needed themselves.

Some people did not like to depend on the government for help.

Many islanders left the shelters because they preferred to look after themselves

# Shelters

After the disaster, over half of Montserrat was unsafe to live on. While new houses were built, people needed somewhere to live. But the new houses were built slowly. In fact, even in 1999, hundreds of islanders were still living in shelters.

The shelters were safe from the volcano, but they were often small and dirty. Tents had holes in them, and were blown away by the wind. Metal shelters were very hot to live in, but they were all that some people had to live in for three years.

**refugee**
a person who is taking shelter in a foreign land from trouble in their home land.

Some islanders made their homes in schools and churches, and lived as well as they could. They were very crowded, and got dirty and unhealthy.

People hated living in the shelters because they had no privacy. One said he felt like a **refugee** in his own country. A lot of people had arrived in the shelters with nothing after their homes were destroyed.

# The old and the ill

Montserrat's older people had seen hurricanes, earthquakes and floods in their lifetime. When the volcano threatened to destroy their homes, some of them thought that it was because God wanted it to happen so they didn't move from their homes.

Older people didn't want to leave their homes

Most of the people killed by the volcano were older people. After the disaster, many young people left Montserrat. So it was mainly old, poor and ill people who fled to the shelters in the north of the island. Some of them moved many times, from one shelter to another. They had no money for new homes, so many of them had to stay in the shelters for a long time.

# New homes

Before the disaster, the people of Montserrat had fine houses. Of the 11,000 inhabitants, only 4,000 people stayed on the island after the volcano erupted. They needed new houses, so that they could move out of the shelters and begin new lives.

A patch of land in northern Montserrat where a new community would be built.

Building work began in the north of the island, but it was dry and windy there, and the houses were laid out in rows. Some islanders were unhappy because they didn't like the new houses and the land was not like the green and gentle land of the south which they loved. Unfortunately they had no choice. There was very little land, and they had no money of their own to build houses as they would have liked them.

The new houses were built very close together.

# The plight of the farmers

Some farmers risked their lives to grow fresh vegetables for islanders living in shelters. The disaster had destroyed the best land in Montserrat. Only the north of the island was safe for houses and farming, but the soil was thin and dry, and there was little land for farmers to buy.

Land costs a lot of money, and most farmers had lost all their money and land under the ash clouds. Churches and a charity helped some farmers to grow vegetables again. It was on government land, not the farmers' own land, but it was a start.

# Exile

Many islanders decided to leave Montserrat altogether. Many travelled to Britain in search of a new life. They felt as if they were in **exile** from the island that had been their home, but they had no choice because the island could no longer support them. There were no schools for their children or hospitals if they were ill.

The islanders leaving Montserrat.

Some islanders stayed with families from Montserrat who were already living in Britain. The British government found other people places to stay. They weren't always very comfortable places. Some stayed in skyscrapers, some in old, dirty houses. The unhappy islanders had to find work quickly. They had to find money and proper homes. It was very hard for them.

**exile**

being forced to be away from your home land

The islanders arriving in Britain.

# Life in Britain

But it was not all bad in Britain. The children from Montserrat found that there was lots to learn in British schools, like how to use computers, and there were lots of other subjects to choose from.

*People from Montserrat at work in Britain*

Some of the women got better jobs than they had at home in the Caribbean.

Soon the islanders made their own communities too. They felt that they had a future.

# The future for the "Emerald Isle"?

Back in Montserrat the rebuilding was continuing. People had jobs. People were working hard to build a new island.

Construction workers rebuild the island.

One day the young islanders might return – when there are houses for them to return to, and when there are new jobs for them.

And in time even the slopes of the volcano will be green once more.

# Index

| | |
|---|---|
| advice from scientists | 15 |
| aid from the government | 17 |
| ash | 5, 6–7 |
| Britain | 27, 28–29 |
| Caribbean island | 2 |
| clouds of ash | 6–7 |
| community | 29 |
| danger | 10–11 |
| destruction of the island | 9 |
| eruptions | 4–5, 6–7 |
| escape of the islanders | 8 |
| exile | 26–27 |
| families | 16 |
| farmers | 24–25 |
| government | 12–13, 17 |
| grief | 16 |
| growing vegetables | 3, 25 |
| ill people | 15, 21 |
| jobs | 29, 30 |
| land costs | 24–25 |
| lava | 5 |
| loss | 16 |
| Montserrat | 2 |
| new houses | 22–23 |
| older people | 20–21 |
| population | 3 |
| rebuilding | 13, 18, 22–23, 30 |
| refugees | 19 |
| rocks | 4–5 |
| schools | 28 |
| scientists | 14–15 |
| shelters | 13, 18–19, 21 |
| unhealthy shelters | 18–19 |
| warnings | 10–11 |